GRAMMARS OF HOPE

Winner of the Mark Ritzenhein Emerging Poet Award

poems by

Chana Kraus-Friedberg

Finishing Line Press
Georgetown, Kentucky

GRAMMARS OF HOPE

*To the Spices: Amy, Dina, and Joanna, who have
been there for everything;
and to Megan, who's been there for all of the writing
and many of the events in this book.
Thank you for being my kin in the world.*

Copyright © 2021 by Chana Kraus-Friedberg
ISBN 978-1-64662-438-6 First Edition
All rights reserved under International and Pan-American Copyright Conventions. No part of this book may be reproduced in any manner whatsoever without written permission from the publisher, except in the case of brief quotations embodied in critical articles and reviews.

ACKNOWLEDGMENTS

Huge thanks to Mary Fox for administrating the Ritzenhein, to Alan Harris, Rosalie Petrouskie, and Ruelaine Stokes for being my mentors, and to Cheryl Caesar who convinced me to enter after I'd decided not to. Huge thanks also to Deborah Margolis for letting me use her fabulous artwork for the cover and for drawing with me every week over Zoom since March because "it's good for our brains."

Publisher: Leah Huete de Maines
Editor: Christen Kincaid
Cover Art: Deborah J. Margolis
Author Photo: Rosalie Sanara Petrouske
Cover Design: Elizabeth Maines McCleavy

Printed in the USA on acid-free paper.
Order online: www.finishinglinepress.com
also available on amazon.com

Author inquiries and mail orders:
Finishing Line Press
P. O. Box 1626
Georgetown, Kentucky 40324
U. S. A.

Table of Contents

Grammars of Hope 1

New York 2

Brooklyn Lust 4

Havdalah 5

Jealous God 6

Reading Lesson 8

A House on Fire 9

Sexual Assailant Appointed to the Supreme Court 10

To Deborah, Who Hopes I'm Doing Well on These Gray Days ... 12

Mannequin 13

Eleanor Marx 15

Hunger Games 16

Bearing Cost 18

Panther 19

Enough 21

If I Can't Dance 22

Authorial Intent 23

Twelve Step Meeting 25

Sometimes You Ask Me 27

First Step 28

Pandemic Insomnia 29

Social Distance 30

Elegy to the Pre-Pandemic 31

That Other Kind of Hungry 32

Grammars of Hope

Someone's explanation of
can and *may*
has left brushstrokes on your
little niece's speech;
you are *able*,
someone has told her,
to throw a ball in the house,
but not *permitted*.
Now she uses *may*
for every query:
"May you lift me up?"
"May you give me the red?"
As though all her questions were
curious, small-fingered probes into
possible futures,
aimed, not at us,
but at the universe,
like prayers.

You and I are adults and
our speech is correct, if sometimes
uncertain;
we wrestle with structures
of *can* and *may*,
capacity and permission,
as grown women do.
But I like to imagine
your niece's grammar
as more hope
than mistake,
as though she'd been
shown two limited paths
and refused them both.
That's not enough, and it can't be
all there is,
she might (one day)
say.
May there be…?
There may be
better ways.

New York

I could have loved *a* New York, but not
the one I was born in,
where every election,
no matter who ran,
it was the fierce
Old Testament God who won.

In His service we lived out
infinite separations:
the male from the female,
the Jew from the nations,
the Sabbath day from
other days of the week.
Faith atomized us.
We repelled each other
like raindrops on
a plate-glass window;
each trapped
in grids of surveillance,
each spying for God.

A train ride away, Susan Sontag
and Annie Leibovitz loved each other,
not-quite-silently,
from separate apartments.

>At 16, a friend and I read about
>Greenwich Village.
>We took the train to 14th Street and
>got out, looking for our kin.

Vivian Gornick walked with her Communist mother
through streets of intransigent life.

>The first bookstore
>we saw was crowded with
>dusty chapbooks.
>We didn't know what they were.

At the corner of
Christopher and Gay Streets,

a rainbow was flying;

> The long-haired man
> behind the store counter
> suspiciously
> eyed our
> long skirts
> until we left.

Daniel Berrigan might have
been protesting
out in the rain.

> Outside, accosted by
> a sweaty male poet
> in orange,
> I bought a packet
> of his work to
> escape him;
> we weren't supposed to
> talk to men.

There were communes and co-ops and
women dancing together.

> If there were places where writers
> talked about words,
> we couldn't find them, or they
> were filled with Gentiles in
> bright, spiky Mohawks:
> We never could have joined.

Someone had painted a placard that
said my body was mine.

> We rode the subway silently home;
> perhaps no kin would have us.

I could have loved a city
like that if I could have
found it, if it could
have seen me.

Brooklyn Lust

Backstage before the school concert,
you might braid her hair.
You wouldn't allow your hands,
even for a second,
to stray toward the soft skin
of her bare neck,
but the strands of hair
would entwine with your fingers
like pulsing veins as you worked,
and you'd
feel a tender, insistent ache
in body parts
you weren't supposed to name.
You had no thought for things
going further,
no word you could use,
but you replayed
that image for weeks until
its mystical power wore off,
your hands, the slight warmth
of her back on your breasts,
the parting of her hair.

Havdalah

On summer Saturday evenings in Brooklyn,
the sunset flamed at the sky's edge
over our block,
and the air was hushed and expectant,
like an intake of breath.
Up and down the street, women
counted the stars—three meant that
the Sabbath was over, that we
could open the mail, turn on
the lights, and that soon
the men would be home
from the synagogue,
their dark hats floating in groups
through the street-lamps' weird glow.
Then the week would begin, and the
air would be different—less velvety,
less weighty.
When I was eight,
I liked to wait on our steps
for the stars and my father,
loving that opening threshold
between secular and sacred,
between night and day.
It was a rare border time;
mostly our world was so definite
and godly. *One thing or the other.*
Male or female; black or white.
False or true.

For years after I left,
I forgot about those dusks;
I had to.
One thing or another.
Good or bad,
right or wrong;
to leave or return.
I didn't know how to stand
with my eight-year-old self
on that threshold,
to grieve for
a life and a certainty
I'd never want back.

Jealous God

"Did you wait
for salvation?"
That's what He'll ask me
when I reach the gate,
and He'll ask me in Hebrew,
the verb gendered male,
because in Heaven everyone,
even the angels,
are men.

And I'll say yes because it's
the answer He wants and because
most of the time I do wait,
as I've been taught—
for the world to change or
the Messiah to come or
for someone to love me;
maybe to become a person
who someone could love.
I've learned how to sit in
the blank air between
the clock's seconds, and
if I'm not patient,
at least I've learned to be passive.
I try not to move.

Some days I want
to tear off my body
like a binding cocoon,
shape a life I could live in,
the way other people do;
I could
accept that no horsemen are coming,
that no light will transform me,
that whatever I am will
have to be enough
to move on.

But on those days a mist,
like the breath of a jealous god,
swarms at my shoulders, and

I hear His voice,
bitter, accusing,
as I've been told
it will be:
"Did you *wait* for salvation?
The question isn't whether
you wanted it
or needed it
or hoped for it," He'll say.
"The question isn't
what your life was like,
with or without it.
All I want to know is,
did you do as you were told?"

"Did you wait?"

Reading Lesson

You came back to Hebrew lessons after missing a week.
You'd had an abortion, you said.
Your face was ashen and drained beneath your wool hat;
you told me there'd been a lot of blood.

I barely knew your name,
but you told me about your Jewish boyfriend,
who you knew didn't want a Gentile child,
not even his own.
His family didn't know about you. He didn't know
you'd been pregnant.
You loved him, you said.

I was 19 and shocked into awe
in my modest clothing.
Your boyfriend had slept with a Gentile,
and you were that Gentile;
you'd entered the land of abortion and sex
like a person in a book.
But then I saw the look on your face:
That tense hope of chasing a kindness
always just out of reach.
I breathed in sharply;
I knew how that was.

So I said, "That's really hard,"
and I meant it. I didn't tell you
that women could be
complete on their own
or that love shouldn't be
an altar where you sacrifice yourself.

I didn't know how to say those things
or even to think them. Not then.
Instead, we opened the Hebrew textbook between us,
chanted the vowels out loud as I'd done at age five.
I skipped the page where you'd have read the word
abba, for father.

After that night,
I never saw you again.

A House on Fire

What would you save from
a house on fire?
Before the virus, my
list was always the same:
my cats, five precious books,
my wallet, my phone—
I never imagined being trapped
in a room holding
only those things and others
I never would have chosen to save:
The fear of solitude,
the perpetual, grinding
process of bodily maintenance.
The sound of the news
announcing deaths, like a drumbeat,
over and over again.

I thought that safety would always
be outside the place where I lived—
I never thought to play the game in reverse.
I never asked myself: If I had to hide from
the world,
what would I save?

Sexual Assailant Appointed to the Supreme Court

On a day
the falling rain can't cleanse,
my female colleagues and I
pass each other in hallways,
each of us drawing a string
of tasks in her wake.
If asked, we'd use the word
busy
as though it all mattered,
as though we were purposeful beings
with the right to say yes or no.

But I can see us through the
king-makers' gaze,
scurrying before
their absolute judgement
like prey:
Just bodies for bearing
children and false witness.
Just mendacity
crystallized into sexual form.
Ridiculous
in our ambitions,
as though dolls came alive
to ape,
laughably,
humans (who are men).

This is the scripture of my childhood,
breaking my ribs to fit
that diminishing gaze,
the *confused but tumultuous clamor*[1]
inwardly chanting,

I *must* not, I *must* not,
in a voice that seemed like my own.
As though dissolving myself
could become a kind of defiance.
As though I could horrify power

---

[1] Woolf, Virginia. (1938) Three Guineas. Hogarth Press: London, UK.

by following orders,
subsiding into
a blank body shaking
on a cold tile floor.

When I looked at
my face in the mirror,
I was taught to see
a grotesque obtuseness, concerned
with mere female affairs.
Some mornings I catch
my reflection, and that's who
I see, still.
And I know
I can't trust what I see,
because I still see through
the misogyny of power.
And I know
I can't trust what I see,
because a good woman knows
her mind has no power.
I stand there frozen, some mornings.

Some days, the snake of betrayal
wears my own face.

To Deborah, Who Hopes I'm Doing Well on These Gray Days

On these gray days, I
am driving to work
through a landscape
studded with injustice:
Prison-manufactured license plates,
migrant-picked vegetables,
electric-cooled houses,
unfolding like fans
on both sides of the street.
I don't want to see them,
and I can't help but see them;
I can't help myself
and don't want to.
I can't help anyone.
I don't want to help anyone.
Nothing would help.

On these gray days
I am
flailing within
the thorn fence of my passivity,
(my justification and my compulsion,
my one true love),
sullen as a teenager or
an interrupted pedant.
I fear I am both.
As I drive,
I'm grousing plaintively
under my breath:
This isn't the world I wanted.
This isn't the kind of person
I wanted to be.

Mannequin

The blinding red was everything
you'd expect:
Blood/murder/militancy/violence
spurting forth, breaking open,
the dull smack of skin
on furious skin;
all of that.

On the assembly line,
they poured it thickly over her head,
spreading it evenly over all
the planes of her face;
no shading, just red.
She became a caricature of herself,
a flat model of a human head, a female head,
one of the masses:
Suitable for consumption or crowd scenes, for photo stock.

And they knew all about bright red,
how visceral it was, but still, fast cars,
men buy fast cars, and
it was the color they had,
it flowed best—
a well-painted head
shows no shadows, they said.
In fact, it's satisfying to see
that finished product,
with all unique features
concealed.
A job well done.

They dropped her then in front of a
screen they'd tinted blue,
like a flat facsimile of the winter sky or
milk mixed with the blank baby blue of
cornflower dye,
for Easter, perhaps. And
they made the screen small because
they knew all that about
blue;
submerging waters and

turquoise with silver
and hope, most of all hope—
they didn't want that,
not really, but it was the color they had.
It set off the uniform red
still wet on her cheeks,
and they made do.
There wasn't too much blue.
You could hardly see it
on the contact sheets
when she was done.

It seems formulaic to say that they didn't
obscure her completely,
but it must have been true.
There's still that one spot,
floating off-center in
the shape of her head:
A streaky green comma,
a wildlife preserve,
a pointillist blue-yellow picnic
like a painting by Seurat.
I don't know if it matters or even
if she knows that
it's there.

If she does,
most days it'll seem
like a defect.
She won't get chosen for crowd scenes—
she'd stand out too much.
But some mornings she'll catch a green
flash in the mirror,
(like gardens and sea glass and jade),
and see for a moment
a less enclosed universe,
a quick lens of grace.

I don't know if it matters,
but I know it will happen.
I know what she'll see.

Eleanor Marx

Dark curly hair escaping
her hat and accompanying pins,
a ferociously wind-whipped woman
speaks from the wooden parade stand,
surrounded by men.
Socialism, she shouts,
means that *more* people
may say:
This is *my* house, *my* coat,
my hat!
A century passes, I hear
the answering roar
at my desk.

There remain now only
the pamphlets she wrote,
hidden in archival boxes;
the strange spotted photo of
a girl in white, posed
like a doll. And the sense of her tenuous
hold on it all—the dream,
the protests, the thousands of workers
marching;
her passionate grasp always just
slipping
from the annals of history,
from her house,
from her hat.

Hunger Games

Every night we
scrambled hurriedly
out of our clothes on
opposite sides of the bed.
Sometimes
I thought I should
unbutton your shirt,
at least,
but I wasn't sure how;
I'd lost the capacity
for unashamed hunger,
if I'd had it at all.

In the daytime,
we lived in the death lab
of your daughter's illness;
our smallest errors could
shatter invisible test tubes,
detonate toxic explosions,
melt our skin or hers.
We'd read everything about
chemical warfare, but it wasn't enough;
even breathing was dangerous.
I lived in
the endless remorse of the
half-second after,
irrevocable time.

I thought I should
undress you
at night,
but I wasn't sure how or
what walls I might crush,
what wholly avoidable disaster
would torment me
the next day.
I touched you as one prays
in a bombed-out
church, kneeling amid
brilliantly-colored splinters
of stained glass.

I'd failed you so often;
I didn't want you to know
you were always
alone in that bed.

Bearing Cost

I envied you the way
I kept talking to you
when you were
too lost
in sadness
to answer.
For you, I was just the
least urgent of
a multitude of claims.
If I'd let myself
vanish into that darkness,
collapse dead-faced
on the unwashed
sheets of our bed
the way you did,
I knew you couldn't
have found me.
Our relationship was a
luxury
you could barely afford.

Panther

I wanted to love you
the way other animals love,
sleek and contained inside their
furred skins,
licking each other
with placid, affectionate tongues.
I dreamt of strolling together
down smooth forest trails;
we'd go home, and
I could learn, I thought,
to be gentle,
to hang up my brace of claws
like a sword on the wall.

But beneath it all
my bastard anger
ground on.
Every night
I snarled and slashed
in my sleep
until both of us woke up afraid;
I comforted you by
saying I dreamt
of old battles.
But every night I lied.
I always was dreaming
about you.

When we woke in the morning,
I always hoped you would
shame me,
but it was like you'd forgotten
the night or like
I'd been there alone.
I'd bare the soft sack of my belly
and wait
for you to gash it open;
you'd pretend
not to see.
One morning you said,
"I don't know why

you think that
I'll hurt you;
I'm not mean,
I'm not that kind of
feline."

I didn't reply,
"But I am."

Enough

After Ada Limon, "The End of Poetry"[2]

Enough of grief and repeating, obsessions and ruptures,
enough of asking myself is this a pattern,
who will I
love and can I ever be loved, whose feeling is this,
Enough.

Enough of fractures and dependence and furies,
of writing poems
with or without truth, with or without anger:
Have I hurt you or have I not hurt you,
what was it that you didn't say that I should have heard,
what was it that I told you that you never heard,
whose thoughts are these, whose privacies are these,
if I'm too heavy for you, will I be too heavy
for anyone, how can I
carry myself, and is it worth it to carry myself,
whose faults are these, whose losses are these,
if I shrink myself small enough, can I
prevent them?
Enough.

If I could want something simple, I'd
look out the window and want it.
If I could wrap myself up in the flannel of silence,
I would. If I could speak words and have
them hold meaning, then I would speak them.
But this shame, this symbol
of failure, is all I can have of you,
so I hold onto it tightly.
Unlike me, it's an object, it still casts a shadow.
But it isn't
enough.

---

[2] New Yorker (April 27, 2020). Web. Accessed April 27, 2020.

If I Can't Dance

In my ideal romantic encounter,
I am a book on a shelf
in an academic library.
Not a book people take out
a lot—one about
Emma Goldman, the anarchist,
covered in library binding
of a strangely appropriate red.

A woman comes down the aisle between
the movable shelves—
maybe I'm not what she's looking for,
but she sees me and picks me up
the way some women
pick up dates
in lesbian bars.
Probably she doesn't even open me.
Maybe all she does is run one finger
down my spine, to touch
the grooved print of my title,
and for an instant she sees Emma Goldman
exploding into skirt-twirling fury
at the anarchist ball:
"If I can't dance, I'm not *coming*
to your revolution!"
It's like meeting a friend
or a fiercer, prouder self
there in the stacks.

Probably the woman doesn't take me out.
She puts me back on my shelf, but she
walks away smiling
because she's seen Emma Goldman.
And on the shelf, I am smiling
because I showed her
Emma Goldman.
And it doesn't matter to either of us
that she barely thought of me,
in my library binding,
at all.

Authorial Intent

I want to be a poet
who chases the perfect sentence,
whose desk hosts a panoply of
possible metaphors waiting
to be called by their names.
I want to pace through my days like
a maniac artist, a prophet
muttering verse to myself
in the streets,
to dream of silencing
hands on my mouth
and wake myself up shouting,
"Bifurcated! Lucid!"
over and over again.

But some days life
feels like a playground
of untethered meaning.
You tell me something is
"sickening," and I want to ask
if you mean
that you feel sick,
or if you think that one should,
or if you have some other feeling entirely, but
"sickening" has an adamant, exceptional sound,
with that hard, solid K in the center.
You say the flowers were "pretty,"
and I want to ask, do you *think* that they are,
or is it something
in your eyes that tells you?
Is "pretty" a feeling?
I can guess what I should
find pretty,
I don't know how to feel.

I want to be a poet who
works toward
that one perfect sentence,
who'd know it
if she saw it—
and in the arena of language,

I've never truly doubted
that I would.
But lately I wonder
how a sentence survives
in the wild.
I could take it outdoors in
my pocket, speak it and see all
the words strung together like small shining orbs;
and I'd know what I meant,
why I'd placed them that way.
I'd know why I said it.

I can't guess what you'd hear.

Twelve Step Meeting

My name is
Terry,
my name
is Joshua, and
my name is Kate, and I'm
an alcoholic,
cross-addicted,
just listening today. I'm,
what I'm grateful for is,
I rode the bus here
and no creepers creeped,
you have to let go
of the stupid bullshit
so you can worry about
the other bullshit.
I can see my daughter
for four hours tomorrow but
that's better than no hours.
My sponsor said,
you have to accept,
he said, look on page 417
in the Big Book.
I'm just trying to
work but
not socialize with
them, you know? Just,
times when I go to
church, when there's
God in my life, it was
like the pastor was looking
right AT me, and I said,
didn't I say?
to my sister,
I'm grateful I'm not
dope-sick today, and
I know I'm not going to use, but
if my boyfriend does...
They wanted to know
when I'm coming back.

I didn't know it would
feel like that,
all that pain with
no drugs to put on it—
I can't handle your feelings, I said,
I can
barely handle
my own.

But I'm grateful
for this chair
I'm sitting on,
I know if I stop being grateful,
what happens,
people who don't
have shit not being
grateful for
what they do have.
I'm not going back,
I know I have to accept
where I am because I'm
sober today, and that's,
I said to him, that isn't
gonna fly, but today
I remembered, I was on the bus
and I remembered...
Can you read that thing
from the book again?
I'm comfortable with
where I'm at even
if other people aren't,
you know what I'm saying?
You know, right?

You know
what I'm saying.

Sometimes You Ask Me

Sometimes you ask me
what the day holds,
and I imagine it like
a pair of cupped hands,
waiting to be filled
in the sharp morning air.
I almost want to tease you a little,
to say that I notice
your use of this phrase,
but I'm afraid you'd stop saying it.
I like how it turns time into
something eager and
open and empty,
like the sky
suffused with
rising light
in the morning.

First Step

After years of playing God
like a slot machine,
(come on, come ON!)
I stand here slicing apples
on Rosh Hashanah eve.
I both believe and do not believe
that we will have a sweet year
if we eat them.
I still want us to eat them.
In one hand I clasp
a ferocious desire
to protect,
like a round, burning stone.

So tonight I'll chant blessings
you don't understand
and I barely remember,
cite the will of the God
of our fathers, as though either we
shared one father,
or our fathers
shared one god.
And I'll believe/not believe
that these spells
could nudge the
inking fingers
of fate.

We'll sit on the couch,
I'll pass you the honey,
and I'll want to say:
I know this ritual,
I speak this language,
I know a guy. In
the old Jewish Bronx,
someone
owes me a favor.
I can get us
sweet years.

Pandemic Insomnia

Behind closed eyes, my body becomes
a display of advice in disaster;
headlines scrolling
up through my thighs and
over my belly
like a stray procreational urge.
Sixty things kids can do
while in quarantine.
Ten myths about
the coronavirus.
Seventy presidential
lies about the coronavirus.
Fifteen tips for
teaching your courses online.

Six reasons
we won't provide hourly workers with
sick leave.
Twelve sewing patterns for face masks,
(nurses not allowed
to use face masks,
nurses fired for
using face masks),
Five apps for mothers
working from home.
Deaths spike in New York.

Twenty-three ways to livestream the opera.
Fifteen livecams of animals
in empty zoos...
I'm not afraid; I don't think
I'm afraid, but that constant chatter,
voices broadcasting from the small
lighted squares of their
isolated rooms—
even if I could sleep,
that Greek chorus wouldn't.
Even if I could sleep,
there'd still be the world.

Social Distance

1.   I visit Allison and Chloe in their yard,
six feet between my lawn chair and theirs.
Allison says she's ready
to be done being pregnant;
I can see the baby shifting and pushing
beneath her shirt.
"We'll have distance socializing when
it's born," Chloe says.
(The virus will be over by *then*, I think).
"I'll hold it up, and it will wave to you
across the gap."

2.   Their son is two weeks old.
The quarantine is three months old.
I go to their yard to meet him from six feet away.
They're tired but loving,
passing his tiny wrapped form
between them
with newly skilled hands.
I can barely remember
how we all used to touch each other,
like that,
or even whether we did—
the bodies of others all seem
so long ago.

When I leave, Chloe
holds up the baby
at my car window,
just like she said
she would, so I can
see him up close.
For a moment, the window frames
them like a snapshot of normal:
New mother
with child.

Elegy to the Pre-Pandemic

What shocks me now
is how many strangers there were.
Each day we collided with
countless people we didn't know,
dragging children past toy aisles or
opening Tupperware at lunchtime,
hefting backpacks over their shoulders while
walking to class. If they had names,
we never expected
to know them. The city clicked with
parallel, impervious movements,
like a table of windup toys,
each intent on its task.

And we were so nonchalant
about it all!
If you'd asked us at night,
we wouldn't have mentioned half
the shoulders we'd brushed
in the daytime.
We didn't expect to grieve
serendipity later, as one
grieves
a bombed-out city:
Its demolished turquoise mosaics,
its surprise intersections,
its still-unformed
friendships or loves.
We didn't imagine
sitting on our couches, in a silence
like mourning,
when the only strangers in sight
were our isolated selves.

That Other Kind of Hungry

> *Because I could not stop for Death—*
> *He kindly stopped for me—*
> *The Carriage held but just Ourselves—*
> *And Immortality.*
> *(With apologies to Emily Dickinson)*

I don't imagine that Death
would stop long for me,
not even if I flagged her down with a razor
or promised that my bones
wouldn't wander
when she was done.
"They're compliant;
They're not beautiful, but
they'll do what you want,"
I'd bargain.
You say that
to everyone,
she'd say.
It never works out.

She'd examine my face
with a fast, fluid glance
from her saddle.
You're that other kind of
hungry ghost,
she'd judge.
You ask for too much,
but you always want
the wrong thing.
"I want you," I'd mutter,
and right then I would;
I'd imagine huddling into
her warm, solid back.
You don't want me,
you want to be beautiful,
she'd say. *You're kind of a ghost already.*
I'd nod and press on:
"Then you might as well take me."

But she'd shake her head.
My heart just wouldn't be
in it, she'd decide,
scanning the sky
for the souls of more
truthful women.
She'd dig a heel
into her horse's flank and
click her tongue twice.

Even Death, she'd advise,
as she rode away,
*wants to be loved
for herself.*

Chana Kraus-Friedberg is the winner of the 2020 Ritzenhein Emerging Poet Award. She grew up in an ultra-Orthodox Jewish community in Brooklyn, New York, where she got her BA at Brooklyn College. Since leaving that community at the age of 20, she has earned a Ph.D. in archaeology from the University of Pennsylvania and an MS in Library Science from the University of North Carolina-Chapel Hill. She has taught academic writing and anthropology to university students and humanities (reading and history) to GED students.

She currently lives with three feline companions in Lansing, Michigan, where she is a health sciences librarian at Michigan State University. She has written poetry since approximately the age of 7, with a decade-long hiatus before moving to Lansing. She started writing again after finding the open mics and poetry community in the Lansing Poetry Room, for which she is deeply grateful. She currently sits on the board of the Lansing Poetry Club. This is her first chapbook.

www.ingramcontent.com/pod-product-compliance
Lightning Source LLC
LaVergne TN
LVHW041601070426
835507LV00011B/1227